The Colony of New York

Daniel R. Faust and Amelie von Zumbusch

PowerKiDS
press.

New York

Published in 2015 by The Rosen Publishing Group, Inc.
29 East 21st Street, New York, NY 10010

Book Design: Chris Brand

Photo Credits: Cover PhotoQuest/Archive Photos/Getty Images, pp. 5, 15 © The New-York Historical Society; p. 7 Hulton Archive/Staff/Getty Images; p. 9 (inset) © Bettmann/Corbis; p. 9 © Granger Collection; p. 11 © Corbis; p. 12 (inset) © Lee Snider/Corbis; p. 13 Library of Congress Geography and Map Division, Washington, DC; p. 19 Interim Archives/Contributor/Archive Photos/Getty Images; p. 21 © Francis G. Mayer/Corbis.

Library of Congress Cataloging-in-Publication Data

Faust, Daniel R.
The colony of New York / by Daniel R. Faust and Amelie von Zumbusch.
p. cm. — (Spotlight on New York)
Includes index.
ISBN 978-1-4777-7334-5 (pbk.)
ISBN 978-1-4777-7286-7 (6-pack)
ISBN 978-1-4777-7327-7 (library binding)
1. New York (State) — History — Colonial period, ca. 1600-1775 — Juvenile literature.
2. New York (State) — History — Revolution, 1775-1783 — Juvenile literature. 3. New York (N.Y.) — History — Colonial period, ca. 1600-1775 — Juvenile literature. I. Faust, Daniel R. II. Title.
F128.4 F38 2015
974.7— d23

Manufactured in the United States of America

CPSIA Compliance Information: Batch #WS15RC: For further information contact Rosen Publishing, New York, New York at 1-800-237-9932.

Contents

New Netherland

For hundreds of years, Native Americans were the only people who lived in the area that later became New York. Then, in 1609, an English **explorer** named Henry Hudson arrived in North America. Hudson had been hired by the Dutch East India Company to find a faster way to reach Asia by sea. Hudson's voyage led to the Dutch claiming the land that would be called New Netherland.

In 1614, Dutch **traders** built a trading post on the Hudson River near present-day Albany, called Fort Nassau. The fort was abandoned three years later because of spring floods. To strengthen their claim to the region, which the English also claimed, in 1624, the Dutch West India Company settled small groups of **colonists** on the Connecticut and Delaware Rivers, on the Hudson River at today's Albany, and on present-day Governors Island, adjacent to Manhattan. Also in 1624, the company built Fort Orange, an important fur-trading post that was where Albany is today.

Native Americans had lived in what is now New York State for hundreds of years before the Dutch arrived. This picture shows a nineteenth-century artist's idea of the first meeting between Henry Hudson and the Native Americans.

5

The English Take Over

In 1626, the Dutch purchased Manhattan Island from the Munsee Indians. The Dutch established the settlement of New Amsterdam on the island's southern tip. It became the West India Company's **administrative** center in New Netherland. At first, most **settlers** in New Netherland were employees of the company. The furs the Indians traded at Fort Orange were sent downriver to New Amsterdam. There, furs and other **raw materials** were loaded onto ships and sent to the Dutch Republic. Over time, New Netherland's **population** grew and farming became more **profitable** than fur trading.

New Netherland was surrounded by English colonies in New England, Virginia, and Maryland. The English established settlements in Connecticut and Long Island, two regions that the Dutch also claimed. In 1660, Charles II became king of England. He wanted to gain more control over North America and to break the hold that the Dutch had on trade in the Atlantic. In 1664, he granted his brother, James, Duke of York, New Netherland.

The Duke of York sent British soldiers to capture New Netherland. The Dutch **surrendered** without a fight. New Netherland was renamed New York in honor of the Duke of York. England now claimed most of the land in North America inland from the Atlantic coast.

This image shows an artist's idea of the Dutch surrender of New Amsterdam to the British. Petrus Stuyvesant, the last director of the Dutch colony, can be identified by his wooden leg. The flag depicted is that of the Dutch West India Company.

Governing New York

The first English governor of New York was Richard Nicolls. Under the 1664 Articles of Capitulation, the English agreed to let the Dutch colonists keep most of the rights they enjoyed under the Dutch **constitution**. When Charles II granted the colony to his brother, that made New York a **proprietary colony**.

In 1673, the Dutch recaptured New York and New Jersey. The next year, they traded them back to the English in the Treaty of Westminster. Charles II died in 1685. The Duke of York became King James II of England, making New York a **crown colony**. James decided to make New York part of a larger colony called the Dominion of New England, which included present-day Maine, Massachusetts, Vermont, New Hampshire, Rhode Island, Connecticut, New York, and New Jersey. He sent Edmund Andros, who had been governor of New York from 1674 to 1681 and whose imperious manners had alienated many colonists, to govern the new colony. Andros was an unpopular leader.

When King James II was removed from England's throne in 1688, Andros was imprisoned in Boston and there was an **uprising** in New York. The New York uprising is known as Leisler's Rebellion, after **militia** captain Jacob Leisler, who oversaw the government between 1689 and 1691.

A Brief Description

OF

NEW-YORK:

Formerly Called

New-Netherlands.

With the Places thereunto Adjoyning.

Together with the

Manner of its Scituation, Fertility of the Soyle, Healthfulness of the Climate, and the Commodities thence produced.

ALSO

Some Directions and Advice to such as shall go thither: An Account of what Commodities they shall take with them; The Profit and Pleasure that may accrew to them thereby.

LIKEWISE

A Brief RELATION of the Customs of the Indians there.

By DANIEL DENTON.

LONDON,

Printed for *John Hancock*, at the first Shop in *Popes-Head-Alley* in *Cornhil* at the three Bibles, and *William Bradley* at the three Bibles in the *Minsries*. 1670.

King James II

This picture shows the first page from a booklet published in London in 1670. It is one of the first descriptions of New York written after England took control of New Netherland from the Dutch.

9

The Fight for New York

By the late 1600s, both England and France had colonies in North America. The French had claimed land in what is now Canada and northern New York, as well as the Mississippi River Basin to the Gulf of Mexico. The British claimed the land east of the Appalachian Mountains and around Hudson Bay, in what is now Canada.

In 1689, a series of wars broke out between England and France. The countries fought for control over North America for nearly 75 years. A lot of the fighting was over New York, because the Hudson River valley and New York Harbor provided access to the **interior** of North America. The final war between Britain and France over North America lasted from 1754 to 1763.

During this war, some Native Americans sided with the British, while others sided with the French. This war became known as the French and Indian War, after the two main enemies of the British colonists. The French and Indian War refers to the North American **theater** of the Seven Years' War, which was being fought in Europe.

This map was created by the French in 1755 during the French and Indian War. It shows the English colonial territories in orange and some of the French colonial territories in green. The pink areas on the map are lands that both England and France claimed.

HUDSON

N BR

Gaspesie

CANADA

NOUVELLE

Abitibis

Lac Alempipon

LAC SUPÉRIEUR

LAC MICHIGAN

LAC HURON

Messesagues

LAC ONTARIO

LAC ÉRIE

NOUV. HAMP. SHIRE

MASSACHUSETS

C. Cod

PENSILVANIE

PHILADELPHIE

VIRGINIE

NORD - CAROLINE

cherakees

C. Hatteras

C. Lookout

SUD CAROLINE

creeks

C. Fear

GEORGIE

Apalaches

Baie des Apalaches

FLORIDE

OCEAN ATLANTIQUE OU MER DU

Explication.

N.B. La province de Main & le territoire de Sagadahook, sont de la jurisdiction de Massachusets-Bay.

11

New York During the French and Indian War

The French and Indian War was fought along the border between the French colonies in modern-day Canada and the Mississippi River Basin and the British colonies. The area included land in the Great Lakes region, the Ohio River valley, and French Louisiana. The British and the French fought for control of all of North America. Many important battles were fought in New York.

The Battle of Lake George in 1755 was a series of small conflicts between British and French forces in northeastern New York. It was the first British victory against the French. In 1757, the French attacked Fort William Henry, a British fort at the southern end of Lake George. The British were **outmatched** and surrendered to the French, who destroyed the fort. The British attacked Fort Carillon, on Lake Champlain, twice. The French drove them back in 1758, but the British took the fort over in 1759. That same year, the British and their Iroquois allies captured Fort Niagara, on Lake Erie. In 1763, the British won the war. France gave up lands in eastern North America to Great Britain and west of the Mississippi River to Spain.

After the British captured Fort Carillon, they renamed it Fort Ticonderoga. This map shows the fort's location on Lake Champlain near Lake George. The small photograph shows Fort Ticonderoga as it looks today.

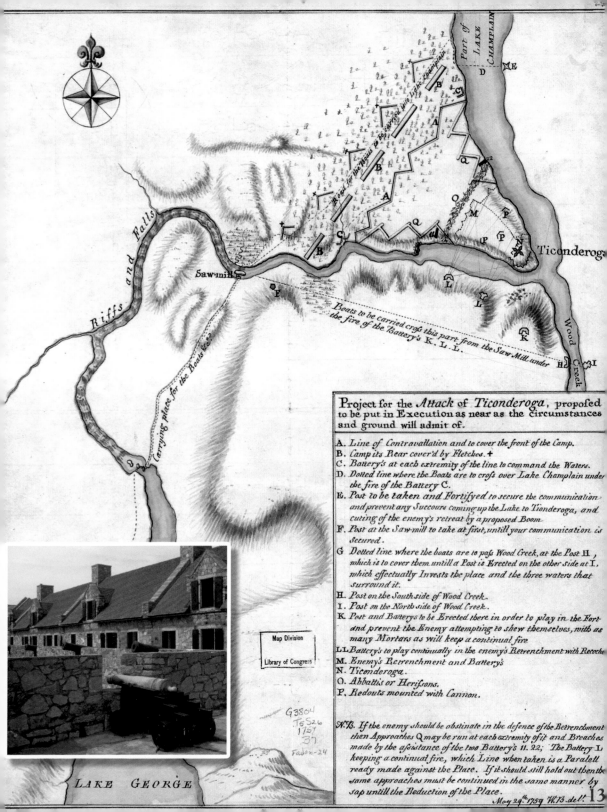

Project for the *Attack* of *Ticonderoga*, proposed to be put in Execution as near as the circumstances and ground will admit of.

A. Line of Contravallation and to cover the front of the Camp.

B. Camp its Rear cover'd by Fletches. +

C. Battery's at each extremity of the line to command the Waters.

D. Dotted line where the Boats are to cross over Lake Champlain under the fire of the Battery C.

E. Post to be taken and Fortifyed to secure the communication and prevent any Succours coming up the Lake to Tionderoga, and cuting of the enemy's retreat by a proposed Boom

F. Post at the Saw-mill to take at first, untill your communication is secured.

G. Dotted line where the boats are to pass Wood Creek, at the Post H, which is to cover them untill a Post is Erected on the other side at I. which effectually Invests the place and the three waters that surround it.

H. Post on the South side of Wood Creek.

I. Post on the North side of Wood Creek.

K. Post and Batterys to be Erected there in order to play in the Fort and prevent the Enemy attempting to shew themselves, with as many Mortars as will keep a continual fire

L.L. Battery's to play continually in the enemy's Retrenchment with Recoche

M. Enemy's Retrenchment and Battery's

N. Ticonderoga.

O. Abbatis or Herissons.

P. Redouts mounted with Cannon.

N.B. If the enemy should be obstinate in the defence of the Retrenchment then Approaches Q may be run at each extremity of it, and Breaches made by the assistance of the two Battery's 11. 22; The Battery L keeping a continual fire, which Line when taken is a Paralell ready made against the Place. If it should still hold out then the same approaches must be continued in the same manner by sap untill the Reduction of the Place.

May 29th 1759 W.B. del.

13

The Colony of New York Grows

When the English took control of New Netherland in 1664, only about 9,000 settlers lived in the colony, which included what is now New Jersey, Delaware, and parts of Pennsylvania. New York City was a small seaport town. By 1771, just eight years after the end of the French and Indian War, the colony of New York was home to about 168,000 people.

Because of the climate and rich soils, New York farmers were able to produce many crops for **export**. New York also has many forests, lakes, and rivers, which provided wood, fish, and a way to move goods throughout the colony. Some people built sawmills to cut lumber for houses and buildings. Others began fishing businesses. Still others opened shipyards to build boats. As more people moved to New York City, it grew. People opened inns, shops, and markets. The city became an important trading center.

This painting shows New York City as it was around 1755. Because New York City was surrounded by water, shipping was important to the growth of the city. Ships carrying furs, crops, and other goods sailed from New York City to Europe and other British colonies, such as Connecticut and New Jersey.

Trade in Colonial New York

England used its colonies in the Americas as a source of raw materials like cotton, timber, and sugar. Raw materials that came from New York included timber, fur, flour, and iron. Raw materials were shipped to England, where they were **manufactured** into goods that were sold in Europe and in the American colonies. English laws limited both what goods colonists could make and what places they could trade with.

English and colonial merchants used several triangular trade routes. These linked England, its American colonies, Africa, and the **West Indies**. Ships carried different things to and from each place. England exported finished goods, such as cloth and guns. The West Indies produced sugar and molasses. Along with raw materials like timber and fish, the American colonies exported rum made from West Indian molasses. Ships brought **slaves** from Africa to sell in the West Indies and the colonies. Though the Dutch brought the first African slaves to New York, the slave trade grew after the English took over.

This map shows one of the triangular trade routes. Not all goods manufactured in Europe were sent to Africa, though. Some were sold back to the American colonies.

Timber, flour, and other
raw materials

Cloth and other
manufactured goods

Slaves

17

Life in the Colony of New York

Even under the English, most New Yorkers continued to follow Dutch traditions and live in Dutch-style houses. In many New York communities, the center of town was the tavern, where colonists could hear the latest news or discuss important issues. Most children learned how to read, write, and do basic math. After that, children in the country worked on farms. Boys in cities were generally **apprenticed** to learn a trade. Wealthy children were often educated by tutors at home. Boys continued their education at Latin schools or abroad.

Most New York colonists were of English and Dutch **ancestry,** but there were several other groups as well, such as people of German, Scandinavian, and African ancestry. In 1991, workers discovered an old African burial ground in New York City. This is helping scientists and historians study how Africans lived in colonial New York. Most were slaves, but some were free men and women.

Under Dutch rule, people were free to practice whatever religion they wished, as long as they did so in private. That tradition continued under the English. Residents of New York were Calvinist, largely Dutch Reformed and Presbyterian, Lutheran, Anglican, Quaker, Baptist, Jewish, and even Muslim.

The Van Cortlandt House, in the Bronx, has been restored to show what it would have looked like around the time it was built in 1748. The brightly painted woodwork and the Delft tiles around the fireplace in this room are Dutch in style.

Colonial Food and Clothes

New York colonists ate traditional European foods, such as pork, cheese, and bread. They also ate Dutch adaptations of Native American foods, such as a cornmeal mush or porridge the Indians called *sapaen,* usually served with milk. Colonial women made stews from meat and vegetables. They cooked the stews in large metal pots over an open fire.

Colonial New Yorkers dressed according to the fashions of England and Holland. Both English and Dutch fashion were **influenced** by the styles worn in the royal court of France. Women and girls wore long skirts or dresses over a shift. A shift was a simple, shorter dress. It helped prevent itching and getting the outer dress dirty.

Men wore frock coats, shirts, breeches, and long socks. Breeches were loose pants that ended just below the knee. Most clothes were made of linen and wool. Only wealthy people could afford fancy cloth like silk.

This family picture was painted around 1772 by an artist named William Williams. It shows a wealthy colonial New York family dressed in the clothing of the time. Lower Manhattan can be seen in the distance behind them.

The Colonists Fight Back!

England spent a lot of money to win the French and Indian War. King George III could not afford to keep British soldiers in the colonies to prevent another war. He made the colonists help pay the cost by taxing goods such as sugar, paper, cloth, and tea. The colonists thought this was unfair because they had no say in making the rules about the taxes. The colonists from New York joined the colonists from twelve of Great Britain's other North American colonies to fight the British.

The **American Revolution** began in 1775. A New Yorker named Robert R. Livingston was a member of the committee that helped write the Declaration of Independence, which announced that the colonies were free from British rule. Colonial leaders adopted this important document on July 4, 1776. Finally, in 1783, the colonists won the war. New York City was chosen to be the capital of the new United States of America until a permanent location could be selected.

Glossary

administrative: Relating to the management of a company or organization.

American Revolution: The war that the American colonists fought from 1775 to 1783 to win independence from England.

ancestry: Family background or history.

apprenticed: Bound to work for another for a period of time in order to learn a trade, craft, or skill.

colonists: People who move to a new place but are still ruled by the leaders of the country from which they came.

constitution: The laws by which a country is governed.

crown colony: A colony ruled directly by a monarch.

explorer: Someone who investigates unknown regions.

export: To send goods to other places to be sold.

influenced: Swayed by the power, taste, or opinion of others.

interior: The inland parts of a country or region.

manufactured: Made by hand or with a machine.

militia: A group of ordinary people who are not soldiers but are trained and ready to fight when needed.

outmatched: Faced a superior opponent.

population: The number of people living in a given area.

profitable: Producing wealth or other gains.

proprietary colony: A colony granted by a monarch to one or more proprietors, or owners, who control the government of that colony.

raw materials: Materials that can be manufactured into goods.

settlers: People who move to a new land to live.

slaves: People who are treated as property to be bought, sold, and forced to work.

surrendered: Gave up possession of something to another.

theater: A region in which key military events, which may be part of a wider war, take place.

traders: People whose business is the buying and selling of goods.

uprising: A localized act of violence in defiance of an established government.

West Indies: A group of islands that separates the Caribbean Sea from the Atlantic Ocean and includes the Lesser and Greater Antilles and the Bahamas.

Index

Primary Source List

Page 9. *Title page from Daniel Denton's pamphlet "A Brief Description of New York."* 1670. Printed for John Hancocks and William Bradley in London, England. There are twenty-two copies of the first edition known to have survived.

Page 11. *Carte des possessions angloises & françoises du continent de l'Amérique septentrionale.* Created by Thomas Kitchen. Engraving. 1755. Now kept at the Library of Congress Geography and Map Division, Washington, DC.

Page 13. *Map of Fort Ticonderoga.* Created by William Brasier. 1759. Now kept at the Library of Congress Geography and Map Division, Washington, DC.

Page 15. *New Amsterdam on Manhattan Island.* Based on engraving by Thomas Doesburgh from Carel Allard's *Orbis habitabilis oppida et vestitus*. Ca. 1700. Now kept at the New-York Historical Society in New York, NY.

Page 21. *The William Denning Family.* Created by William Williams. Oil on canvas. 1772. Now kept at the Smithsonian American Art Museum, Washington, DC.

Websites

Due to the changing nature of Internet links, Rosen Publishing has developed an online list of websites related to the subject of this book. This site is updated regularly. Please use this link to access the list: **http://www.rcbmlinks.com/nysh/nybc**

Faust, Daniel R.

The Colony of New
York.

DATE			